THE DANGER MODEL

THE HUGH MACLENNAN POETRY SERIES

Editors: Allan Hepburn and Carolyn Smart

The Danger Model

Madelaine Caritas Longman

McGill-Queen's University Press
Montreal & Kingston • London • Chicago

ISBN 978-0-7735-5885-4 (paper)
ISBN 978-0-2280-0023-5 (ePDF)
ISBN 978-0-2280-0024-2 (ePUB)

Legal deposit third quarter 2019
Bibliothèque nationale du Québec

Printed in Canada on acid-free paper that is 100% ancient forest free
(100% post-consumer recycled), processed chlorine free

Financé par le gouvernement du Canada   Funded by the Government of Canada   Canada   Conseil des arts du Canada   Canada Council for the Arts

We acknowledge the support of the Canada Council for the Arts.

Nous remercions le Conseil des arts du Canada de son soutien.

Library and Archives Canada Cataloguing in Publication

Title: The danger model / Madelaine Caritas Longman.

Names: Caritas Longman, Madelaine, 1991– author.

Series: Hugh MacLennan poetry series.

Description: Series statement: The Hugh MacLennan poetry series | Poems.

Identifiers: Canadiana (print) 20190139439 | Canadiana (ebook) 20190139447 | ISBN 9780773558854 (softcover) | ISBN 9780228000235 (ePDF) | ISBN 9780228000242 (ePUB)

Classification: LCC PS8605.A7525 D36 2019 | DDC C811/.6—dc23

This book was typeset by Marquis Interscript
in 9.5/13 Sabon.

CONTENTS

SOMETHING LIKE LIVING

I feel like I was dropped into the middle
of my personality years ago & I've been trying to get
to the edge ever since....is this the edge?

Carrie Fisher via Twitter, May 2, 2014

WHITE INFINITY NET

For Yayoi Kusama and Jill Bolte-Taylor

Snow touching snow. Petal and rhizome,
    asterisk, osteocyte. Splitcell and starry
    matrix of bone

        a sharp pain behind my left eye   insomnia prickles
    bright as ice cream   body out of bed
                            to paint
Once I awoke I could not walk, talk,

                      the single blanket
    read, write   drips its pattern
    the river's white stones   like milk   across the floor
                I got on my cardio glider

I could not recall any details of my life   frost climbs the broken window
                        onto a hand
        monochrome net
                American emptiness
          space extending   all directions
it gripped me. and it released me. and it gripped me.
                      O'Keefe's cow bones
      a vertigo of   open sky

and released me. no longer the choreographer of my life

    the crinkle of light on water decided   I might
                      become a farmer
  my consciousness shifted   and paint on the side
               it was beautiful there
     by the underlying surfaces

my unrecognizable hands

to some esoteric space, witnessing myself

fetal ball in an ambulance

two planes crossing   *"We do not treat illnesses like yours*
at Bellevue"

the dialogue inside   white sound of water

either the doctors
would rescue my body
texture of paint   *or this was a moment*
striking the tub   *of transition*

canvas visible beneath

the myelin   pollen and fractal

mycelium threading outward   to materialize rapture

tens of thousands of arcs
crawling off the canvas
the atoms and molecules of my arm blended   onto the table
with the atoms and molecules of the wall   onto the floor
and my body
gathered around
could no longer define the boundaries
invisible points of gravity
microscopic lights   accumulating mass
hundreds of millions   of white pebbles
"What makes it even more terrifying –"
"Remarkable. Not terrifying – remarkable."
each individually verifiable   really "existed" there

4

the stones' white spirits

the brain stem potential

the riverbed

for death   where she hid

nets of light   from her family

monochrome obsession   the grackles' human voices

into consciousness

the ash of paintings fell
like the ash of flowers

respect for the cells composing   repetition compulsion
a human form   stage or trap

tightrope, safety net

blood clots   flowering water
in the fibres of language
between meaning and sound
forty-five hours   dissolving

English   into white

thirty-seven years   into white

painting from pre-dawn   *I had to relearn the words*
into deep night   *for peanut butter, for tuna fish*
                             to describe what was happening
                             inside my body

enveloped

the single particle of light

I didn't know if there was anybody I was supposed to be mad at
    before it was all gone

        that was my life

"Are there mysteries of the brain that are better left unsolved?"
"No."

TRANSFORMATIONAL IMPULSES

I suppose I had always hoped that, through an act of will and the effort of practice, I might be someone else, might alter my personality and even my appearance, that I might in fact create myself, but instead I found myself trapped in the very character that made such a thought possible and such a wish mine.

Lyn Hejinian, *My Life*

One self prunes violently
at all the others
thinking she's the gardener.

Jenny Xie, "Tender"

ALONE IN HOTELS

this room could be anyone:
    fluorescent and scentless

a white box cut
    into black city sky

        any city. any sky.
           same night static

   and discontinuous –

      the room comes
        into being.

rewind. repeat.

    the night's cold
      meets a palm

    on the glass

  let it fall

       the room comes
         into being.

  smudged light hovers
    over skyline and highway

headlights catch   and turn   fade

     into washroom's white gleam
        into cubicle basin

        steam up the mirror
        so as not to have a face

this room could be anyone
     blank in the steam

water uncurls
     pulling smoke from hair

     towels soft

        as no touch at all

unsmudge
     undo

        fall

     the lines of a body
   unbend

        and lengthen

into white sheets
     into dark
        the room comes
     into being

into dream

with no narrative

until you drift
                towards yourself

not so much waking

as deciding

to resume –

PETROCAN

Dismantle yourself in a gas station bathroom. Curl soap
around your tongue and scrape the sleep from your eyes.
Swipe your hands down your jeans and breathe
the sanitized fluorescence. Close the door behind you.

Pick up the drink that will leave your hands shaky
and a twinge in your teeth. Supervise your fingers
as they maneuver coins hand to hand, then crush
the receipt to the corner of your pocket. Smile.

Walk outside. Shake out your fingers, petroleum stains
that have hardened into the lines of your knuckles.
The landscape boils flat with afternoon. Above the asphalt,
white dust dilates, an ache of sun twitching under your nails.

Sit in the dry grass and watch the pavement waver.
Let your throat itch with shards, broken mirrors
and vacuum cleaners. In the bleached length
of summer, notice your skin strain

like chapped sidewalks. How your tongue drags
with noises you can't touch to sound. Traffic surges,
a whisper through sheets of dull sky. Every red car
pierces your eyes.

Inhale the dust. Shift your gaze down,
past shoelaces and words. Between traffic,
dark birds weave their shapes through the intersection,
clutching the updraft. They carry the shape

of their passing, jewel the air with speech older than yours.
Behind your breathing, listen. This may be important.

broken sunrise
        a crow drips
from the rooftop

ROOM WITHOUT WALLS

a woman stands beside an unfinished chair

raw plywood   hammer in hand

     cells of light line the curtains

opening   into white space

         the walls undreamed

she holds her body like it is no enemy

      and looks into me

i want this:

      eyes like the sun

tremble of nerves in the present

     how she changes

           the room

      like light

but my eyelids unshutter

     breath heavy as water

the wings of my heart a trapped bat

       as i gasp back   into myself

       the poem of her presence

shreds

       its full moment folds

       of cotton to shoulders

          the fabric of her jeans

       the silence that said

everything is here

       in this room without walls

i don't know if she was someone i loved

       or someone i was

the way in a dream everyone

       is someone else

tall grass
our one shadow
waving

*It is not the artist's intention that the performance should
be repeated.*

In Rhythm o, Marina Abramovic absents herself
      Rose, whip, perfume, blue paint, scalpel, apple,
from herself, positions her body as exhibit.
      bread, comb, fork, honey, wood,
Does not invite violence, but leaves it open as an option,
      hairbrush, scissors, wine, grapes, nails,
which some critics say is enough to call invitation,
      axe, sugar, soap, pocket knife,
call narcissism, call exhibitionism. And I'd rather
      chocolate cake, chains, olive oil, salt,
not be writing another catalogue of harms, not trying to define
      feather, bullet, pistol, Band-Aid,
a position to justice/the world by what hurts, constructing
      book, bell, candle, mirror,
(call it life or identity)
      alcohol, medal, leather strings, yarn,
by what I cannot tolerate. Like saying, today
      drinking glass, cotton, shoes, chair
I read half of an article on how women's (it's usually women's)
      safety pin, hair pin, red paint,
self-destructive behavior makes sense if we understand
      hammer, paper, kitchen knife,
emotions as objects, as *real*, regardless of
      dish, wire, camera, needle
if they're deemed appropriate. Meaning, perception of harm
      box of razor blades, water, sulfur, hat

is itself harm. And I didn't want to read that, wanted
metal pipe, scarf, handkerchief, white paint,
to read that I could become anyone if I really tried, wanted
lamb bone, stick, newspaper, saw,
to read that I could exist just enough inside my body
flute, metal spear, bandage,
to use it as escape hatch. Kindness exists, I know,
spoon, coat, flowers, matches,
how nothing cancels out anything else. How one person
pen, lipstick
in the audience lifted the gun and curled
rosemary branch.
Abramovic's finger over the trigger, made Abramovic press
There are 72 objects
the barrel to her own head, and I know
on the table
other people stopped them, shouted and threw
that can be used on me as desired.
the gun out the window, and I hate writing
Performance:
about guns even if it's putting them down and I can't even
I am the object.
listen to that Tori Amos album all the way through, just replay
During this period
that song where she sings, *This is not really happening*
I take full responsibility.
then sings, *You bet your life it is, you bet your life it is, you bet
your life it is, you bet your life.*

INTERLUDE: PARKING LOT

"You'll laugh about it someday." And I do. The picture of me,
purple lipstick and a pirate hat, solemnly holding a lemon.
On the backyard stairs, I sulk proud in my goth dress
and pink feather boa, insist to my baffled father, "It's for *art*."
Uncomprehending, he snaps the shutter. Allows me to remain.

Leave me these snapshots. Leave me whisper-reading
the Chapters erotica section, my friends and I laughing
because we're the first to discover sex and its inelegance.
The adrenaline hum when J shoplifts, our ears drumming,
convinced we'll go to prison over *Italian Stallions*.

Leave me the weeklong relationship where we held hands once.
Leave me the tremble of touching, of being wanted. Hair catching
in our lip gloss. Leave me in the theatre, pulling the loose thread
from my best jacket, placing it on the bald head in the next row,
convinced this is somehow impressive.

Leave me my black pants with chains and zippers,
my bracelet with tentacles. Leave me by the river with B,
crossing the bridge by Chinatown, in the wrong place,
the place the cars go, they're coming towards us,
leave us running, laughing so we won't panic.

Leave me a mind never overwritten by calorie counts
or lethal dosages. Leave me never giving my number
to the man twice my age who asked on the train,
because I was fifteen and too scared to lie.
My parents that night, angry to cover up their fear.

Leave me the laughter before it turns mean.
Before Meg from *Family Guy* swallows a bottle of pills
and the dialogue pauses to show it's a joke.
Before the stomachaches are diagnosed as internal bleeding
and the anxiety is diagnosed as anxiety.

Leave me behind the Chinook Centre parking lot,
on top of a mountain of soot and snow, laughing
with my friends beneath a sky of light pollution.
Just leave me something. Some way to say,
before my throat closes, I'm still here.

through the train window
LOVE ME in ten-foot letters
we ride in silence

I can never confess enough to come clean. I trace
the stitches of stories, tongue the itch inside words
where meaning should be. Night deepens and I nudge
into the shifting space of memory, make myself a joke
stretched to trembling. Jab my nails into self-deprecation
long after the laughter has ceased. The party desaturates

into the streets, and I remain, throat furred with red wine.
Bolting the door, I walk like walking is sleep. Unable
to lie still in the socket where a thought used to be.

If the past is an essay, I have erased. Rewritten tone from anecdote
to cataclysm to *i don't remember.* I wear holes in the pages.
Hit refresh on a Facebook page waiting to see what she will do.
Forgetting the face looking back is my own.

Alone, I watch the window drift over the room.
The same moon shivering. I boil to the surface, skin slick
with fever, try to sweat myself out.

I don't want to be an earthquake. Okay. Sometimes. I push
the wrong side of sunrise, sharpen the sky to a slap.
Drink in that light, glassy, desolate. Try to break like a wave
or a phone screen. In this narrative, I can make myself
victim or villain, inspiration, caution tape, chemical,
machine. I cannot trace my way to the spaces between.

*i was devastated because you left to buy groceries. i was
devastated because you are better than me.* There is such a

thing as too much hunger, or the wrong kind of hunger. Like:
I feel too big for me. Like: *if i could just explain clearly enough –*

How can you ask a question that you live inside?

As though guilt could be enough. Could glue the days together
with to-do lists or apologies. I seek contact but flinch
when I'm touched. Everyone I've loved I have thanked
for putting up with me.

i will say something inappropriately sad, then shake with laughter
to balance out the mood. i will drink enough to tell you everything
and to take it back in the morning. Closeness as plausible
deniability. Honesty as: *i might be making this up.*

I try to place myself in this body, a holding cell for strangers
who speak in my voice. In a notebook, I scribble divisions
between future and present, past and dream, try to trace a path
to human. To five-year plans and favourite TV shows.
Something to offer. Something to hold.

In the shower, I rub heat into my nerves, remember a filmmaker
who said he shot violence black-and-white because the real pink
of blood in water never struck the right tone. Looked femmey
and flippant, an off-colour joke. I scrub my skin new
with apple soap, watch water stir green before it bleeds
back to nothing. Step out into morning, shaking in my sameness.

At the edge of the bed, I anchor myself to this chill.
To the sound of rain. In a one-room apartment with a storm
outside, I try to fill my body. I press my palm to the window
and let the weather rattle.

stars between
the winter branches –
this strange homesickness

So I drank red wine and it wasn't enough. So I drank Red Bull
       and it wasn't enough. So I talked very quickly
about food and travel and wanting to live
everywhere and learn every language and once I'd done
everything on earth, how I'd become an astronaut
                      or astral projectionist –
but talking didn't empty me.

      So I slept for days, but silence didn't fill me.
So I scrubbed my skin and pulled the dye from my roots
      but I was still left with myself. So I wrote emails
to organizations for the desperate, and volunteers all named Jo
said that sounds very hard
                and we are not authorized
to give advice in these situations
      and please write again,
              anytime.

So I ate or didn't eat. So I slept or didn't sleep.
"So tell me about yourself" was a test I couldn't pass
             and couldn't study for

and I wondered
     what I would want
if I could want something.

A stain of light hangs over the city: omen or crown. Emerald
    dust
on the night's grey belly. Clouds the colour of stepped-on metro
bubblegum, same starless asphalt above and below. But then:

something. Biohazard or bioluminescence. We call it aliens, angels,
universal tear or potential rapture out of ourselves and this night.
On the wrong side of sunrise, everything's hideous and hilarious,

Beckett-absurd, like *fine, aliens, what-the-hell-ever.*
Shivering in slush, we march blisters into our boots.
The indifferent traffic flickers past like static.

The always-sleepless internet fevers its conspiracies.
Paranormal or billboard? They say the light belongs to Desjardins.
A credit union. A garden in the sky. They want to make a forest
    of the night.

Promise to canopy the winter in green, irradiate the midnight rain.
Glitter up the sleet until it shines like algae. For the office workers,
they say it will be artificial sleep. Will ornament the hours like
    dreams.

Boost mood, vitalize, shoot through their veins like vitamin D.
Dependable, winter-green. Though, some argue, biological
    contaminant.
Warn of misaligned sleep phase, environmental havoc, hormonal

catastrophe. The D D T of our dreams. But there's no law against it, is there, making light? No one owns the clouds. Desjardins brands the night with copyrighted wavelengths. Their very own green.

In the artificial garden, clouds rust into verdigris.
A path through the sky. Emerald eye
that never blinks.

We walk towards it.

the old woman's hands
water sounds
from the koto strings

STRANGELOVE SYNDROME

Also known as *alien hand*. When an arm and its fingers disentangle
thought   from action from intent. The limb reaches out to grasp
what it wants. Unknots   from consciousness, gives body
        to a mind   of its own.

For days or years the hand takes matters   into itself.
Graceless neighbour, unruly roommate, conjoined companion or foe.
Some term this new mind *frightening*. Others *flamboyant*. The hand

wrestles, insistent, disobeys both mind and mate. Some name it
like a child or pet. *Baby Joseph*. Others call it simply *him*.
        The hand tweaks cheeks, unbuttons blouses,

pesters its twin.   Slaps   the cigarette from one's lips.
Guess he doesn't like that. Reverse-phantom, the hand possesses itself
and lives. The split-mind fissure creeps its way down the body:

Good hand. Bad hand. *Anarchic limb*. The brain a bitten peach,
hemispheres split, unblooded necrotic   or starry with scars:
the brain's constant touching of itself   clogged, the body turns

argument. Desires once-unnamed even in thought, the subconscious
        now gropes, strikes, strangles. Unburied,   impulses
clamber into themselves. Will not be shaken. Will not be held.

        Like the heart, the hand wants what it wants
                and wants   and wants   and wants.

Somewhere, a seventy-seven-year-old is settling
into her sofa, into evening news and the strained autumn light
when she catches   a bar of black   winging

across the screen of her vision, feels someone reach out
                                    and stroke her cheek.

[BORDERLINE: TALK]

contents: hide

a complex and abstract term
cannot be depicted by an image

move image
to the text of the body[1]

[image description: a clear empty
in various stages of healing]

positive affects: incongruous gratitude
at perceived expressions of kindness

illicit memory

the mind dissolves
to protect distance

environment / triggers / action potential
the body's map of / itself

spatial coding

---

[1] may align with normal teenage behavior; not diagnosable under age
eighteen unless symptoms have been present for one year

hippocampus (neuroplastic) (seahorse)
may be stunted, affecting
inhibition   ~~memory~~[2]   ~~space~~
difficulty diverging from responses
that have previously been taught

amygdala (almond)
~~memory decision reaction~~
social judgments regarding
other peoples'   faces

~~thought suppression~~

2   some clients do not report any traumatic event

shadows on the moon
the spaces I occupy
but do not fill

ODE TO PESSOA

After I was born they locked me up inside me
But I left
     Fernando Pessoa

      *

Quiet universe, many-tongued, you spun yourself
out of yourself. Turned your own name orthonym.
Omnivorous autodidact, you lost yourself

in language and libraries, dedicated a life
to remaining missing. You are not buried
in the courtyard of Jerónimos Monastery.

Unencumbered by identity, shepherd
of the glossolalic green hills, cascade
of language and rain.

Let the sheep run free.

      *

If what I write has any value, it is not I who am valuable.

In the hands of the grass, your atoms unlink.
All that remains: twenty-five thousand
shambolic pages, long-abandoned Lisbon

apartments, empty chair at the coffee house.
Fervent person, soft-spoken and smoldering,
where have you hidden yourself?

*

You said you would rather think of absinthe than drink it.
A cup of coffee, a cigarette and my dreams
can substitute quite well for the universe and its stars.

Your grandest romance remains a lone,
hasty kiss in the office before returning to work.
Life always pained me, it was always too little.

Of course, none of these voices
are necessarily your own.
You unchain multitudes:

alchemist, astrologer,
theosophist, philosopher,
physician and navigator,

radical inactivist.
Translating yourself across continents
behind the glitter of your spectacles,

schoolboy writing letters to his alter egos.
The world a great book opening
in a language you could not parse.

Always doubting the solidity
of that space men agreed
to call a heart.

*

But what a gift to channel Caeiro's
ordinary ecstasy.

To see flowers and trees and hills
and only see flowers and trees and hills.

Your self only
a part of the landscape.

Merely to hear the wind blow
makes it worth having been born.

We listen for you in the mountains and fields,
your spirit brushing through the dark grass.

You travel so lightly
because you carry nothing
not even yourself.

DEAR VOID

Fey
/fā/
giving an impression of vague unworldliness
having supernatural powers of clairvoyance
fated to die; doomed; marked by a foreboding of death or calamity

Dictionary.com

"Nothing" is
the force that renovates
the world

Emily Dickinson,
fragment written on an envelope

ALL I REMEMBER ABOUT *THE WORLD ACCORDING TO GARP*

there is a little boy who is quiet and distant,   removed
as though he always has his ears under bathwater   so when he drowns
it feels inevitable   because he wasn't
      really part of the story   watching like he knew
he was a character in a book, and by knowing became   separated
      from the narrative,   too self-conscious to be character
so that his quietness became a shadow   leading to his quietude
      so when he died it seemed inevitable   though of course
it wasn't, of course Irving wrote, edited, finalized   the boy's
erasure,   though the boy was so young and so distant/quiet he was
in a way sexless   not so much a boy   as a gap
      in the air   to pour in loss   a silence reminding
the audience   to listen carefully   though i wonder
if Irving hadn't silenced him what the boy would have said
      and whether Irving held him under because he didn't know either
                        dear boy dear void

dear bathwater   how would you narrate yourself after you knew
you were in the wrong story   how does a gap in the air
build a life
become a person   can it   dear absence how can i be more
                        than someone else's loss

For over 50 years immunologists have based their thoughts, experiments, and clinical treatments on the idea that the immune system functions by making a distinction between self and nonself. Although this paradigm has often served us well, years of detailed examination have revealed a number of inherent problems. This Viewpoint outlines a model of immunity based on the idea that the immune system is more concerned with entities that do damage than with those that are foreign.

> Polly Matzinger, "The Danger Model: A Renewed Sense of Self"

To begin, you must believe in a future.

> Louise Glück, "Disruption, Hesitation, Silence"

i.

lexis : speech
thumos : soul, spirit, bond to blood and breath;
        the site of feeling, reaction, desire
        to be recognized
a : a negation

i.

To exist requires immense energy.
Do you permit yourself to exist?
It's not a yes or no question. There has to be how.

The body is not detachable, but it is easier to say, "the body."
To make it not-self, sever
muscle from memory. Membranes keep out
most of the world, absorb what remains.
What cannot be excreted is shaped into tissue
or history. Ulcers in the intestinal wall.
Shoulders that shirk from touch.

Notice I do not say, "my shoulders."

In the morning, trees of red light sink into
my eyelids. Burrs of thought gather
and I become.

i.

First friend, I love you and we are so tired.
Your smell of sweat and cinnamon, threadbare
softness of your coat, and posture woven

against the wind. The snow blows one way,
black sky another.

I glow like a pharmacy, trying to tell you –
            The years expand between us.

Factory work soaks your clothes,
stitches stones to your gestures

when your hands try to talk. Eyes quieted.
We fill our mouths with dollar store chocolate,

pour smoke through our lips
across unbroken snow.

Clouds spill out of us, sink out of sight
in the glass-black sky.

Call it a soul, this hollow glow
throwing back the Christmas lights.

i.

"I don't really care what happens
to my body," she says as we jaywalk
          the Center Street tracks,
her cigarette habit aged from defiance
          into resignation.

          (As we learned from girlhood,
doing up the top button
          before boarding the bus:
we are always being read
          and rewritten.)

Her laugh whitens the air. I joke
about transcending
          this physical finitude,
shoulder blades   opening
                    to a bleach of wings.
A holiness so devastating
it has to be ironic.

In my mind, I peel myself like an orange,
looking for something inside. A core to split
into segments,   , hold out as offering.
Snow falls on snow. Our footprints go blank.

i.

At eighteen I developed an autoimmune disease,
though I say an autoimmune disorder,
a word that sounds cleaner,
less permanent. Something misplaced
rather than lost.
                    My body ceased
to recognize itself. White blood cells target
intestinal tissue, mistaking myself for intruder.

I sharpened my bones on absence.
Cut out oranges, meat, oil, spices. Polite conversation
prefers membranes intact, insides internal.

"Does it hurt?" asks the doctor, moving his hands
over different parts of my abdomen. I don't know
how to answer.

i.

The inability to express anger
may be read as contentment.
The self forms in/around
a negation. In high school
we said we didn't care
about politics, rolled our tights

over knife bites. At fourteen
I kept a rock beside my bed
to smash against my arms.
I don't know why
except that it felt right
or maybe felt wrong
in that good way,
that is, less wrong
than doing nothing.

i.

At fourteen I crumpled
amongst junior high toilets,
writing "fuck" on the walls.
Hardly original,
yet a poem in its pressure.

i.

Is the self inside the body
or is it the body
or can it leave?

An academic calls the body
"a metaphor for the self"
and I – "I" – vibrate.

Seeking an end to metaphor
I use my body to send messages
to myself

to force my attention
or erasure.

i.

Can I call this anger?
Braid its hot metal
into a will? Crackle

a match against "I"'s
black candle, split down my matter
for light to read by?

I forget what is me
in this metaphor:
vision, wick, vanishing point.

i.

I know there must be more
to this time than hostility.
But what I remember
                is always
that rush of air panicked
    out of me, running
        in the snow

until nausea knocked me down.

i.

The psychologist Batja Mesquita writes
that many cultures do not see emotions
as internal processes, but as energies living
between two or more people. A change in the air
when we recognize each other.

We barely exist as individual organisms,
writes psychiatrist Bessel van der Kolk.
Most of our energy is devoted
to connecting with others.

Even self-harm, says sociologist Peter Steggals,
is a social practice: *a letter that has been written*
                                    but not sent, set aside
in a safe place
            with the possibility
                                    that it may be sent in the future
                        with the hope
                        that by then the recipient will be able
                                                to understand.

An anonymous commenter
writes on a message board, *all action*
is communication even if u are only
communicating with yourself.

i.

My roommate told me I would know
if I had been in love, the same way
I would recognize a panic attack.

i.

On paper, alexithymics are
hyper-literal. Numb to nuance,
fixated on the physical; more object
than subject.

But that doesn't sound right.
I can't stop thinking in metaphors.

i.

I changed schools. Changed schools again.
Made friends
        who didn't step away
when we were seen together.

Aspiring artists, which mostly meant
wearing black, making sex jokes,
drinking Sourpuss into sunrise
on front lawns, certain the fire truck
                had come to arrest us.
We burned Barbie's hair for art class, glued jellybeans
and glitter to our faces, always arrived late
        and mostly-always laughing.

The spaces we occupied sparkled and smoked,
each breath that much sweeter
        because we had stolen it.

Existence was rebellion. Snow and slurs
hurtled from car windows, still reaching
for each other's hands. *Is that a boy or a girl?*
Language couldn't hold us, yet we spoke.

Existence equaled rebellion.
We pretended we chose that.

We saw the marks
on each other's bodies
but didn't know what to say.

i.

*An immune response specifically aimed
at self-determinants.*

i.

We swung from monkey bars as frost bit
our palms in the dark, sharp as stars.

Shining with heat in our thin jackets,
we lay on our backs on the ice
and finally spoke
        of how we wanted to die

by which we meant:
how urgent our hunger
for a world we could live in.

i.

I read that certain illnesses
may be the body's way
of insisting on care.
That pain

is a survival mechanism,
a way for the body
to speak:

Are you there?

i.

At eighteen, my mechanisms of being
broke down. Cells violated membranes,
tore tissue to ulcers, read self as infection.

The spring light broke
itself on the concrete. I slept on the couch
by the bathroom, shat blood in secret.

I have never been handled with such delicacy.
Watching my body manoeuvred
between paper gowns and passenger seats,
speaking for itself into stethoscopes.
Pain objective and outside
my control, I was remade
blameless.

The doctor periscoped my insides. I apologized for the mess.

i.

An Amazon review of my favorite author
calls her memoir of addiction *narcissistic,*
obsessive, compulsive. Who is allowed
to say "I"?

Failing to absorb iron, I bruise
on chairs and armrests, places the world
touches me. Comment sections, blunt
voices, ambiguous eye contact.
All of it accusation: another

attention-glutton,
millennial and false.
Capillaries burst
beneath my surface.

I look for these ruptures.
How does one know a boundary
if one does not test it?

i.

I am trying to make you love
or believe me. I am trying
to live in a body.

i.

I collapse into the back of a taxi, laughing and crying
quietly, so as not to disturb the driver. I ask my roommate
to hide the meds when we get home. She promises.
And then I'm in the living room, saying

this isn't really happening, I'm acting, asking
for attention and
I'm sorry.

She brings glasses of water,
their surfaces trembling. Says,
"Who cares if you want attention! Everyone
wants attention! It's part of being a person!"

i.

Is there a difference between a personality and an imitation
of a personality? I want to be honest, but I see the wires.
      There's no polite word
for unbound hunger, so I leave that out, the motivation.
      Polish the absence
into something academic. Malleable, a sculpture of potential.
How it collapses. How it shines.

                    When I meet another

                person like me, the space between us
thins and quiets. Two mirrors reflecting an infinity
of possible selves

                    until someone moves.

NARCISSUS SEA

"My big job is to glimpse my vision. We were born on earth. After all, well ... moon is a polka dot, sun is a polka dot, and then, the earth where we live on is also a polka dot."

   Yayoi Kusama interviewed on Louisiana Channel

You come to make a name for yourself.
Burn the animal-glue of your adolescent paintings,
       cross the sea from Matsumoto to Manhattan.

Your one bedroom apartment clutters
with neurosis and ambition. Sleeping
too little and on a salvaged door, you sew

soft sculptures of phalli and food.
Your fears accumulate on every surface.
       Macaroni crunches underfoot

in your installations. Pasta
consumes shoes and mannequins,
phalli barnacles armchairs and rowboats.

This physical world terrifies you. You take it in,
reflect it back   a thousandfold.
Hang it on the walls,   fill rooms
with your terror. Invite us in to look.

Despair's another artwork,
larger than your life. You survive yourself.
It's more material,
>   though you sleep all day
>   though your hands shake
>   though it's constant tension
>   between swallowing the world
>   and being swallowed.

You see the earth: a pale blue polka dot
in a net of infinity. The ceiling's molecules
>   spin unrestrainedly,
>>   and your every cell dizzies.

You are a pattern on the planet,
>   which is pattern in a starscape
a world in a droplet
>>   in a cascade.

You paint from atop a ladder
>   to reach the scale of your visions.

A polka dot priestess officiating marriages,
painting dots on the bodies of beautiful hippies.
>   You proselytize ego death
>   then sign your name.

Craft infinity in mirrors of water and darkness.
Polka dots swallow food, dresses, assistants,
                sex, politics, the kitchen table,
            sofas and teapots, the books in their cases,
            water in its glass. The TV and microwave
                sleep in the dark, obliterated
into blacklight: this visible world
            which we are not in.

You paint. The space you work in
            swells with eyes and colour, repetitive
                as biological cells.

In Pyeongwa Park, your dogs bark,
                Hello, Anyang with Love.
Their mouths open into polka dots.

You lie down, a part of the *Red Horizon.*

                Invite us into the darkened mirror
                    to step out of ourselves
                    and dissolve,

            to touch the edge
            of the hallucination, where dream
        is made real:

            no line
between total control
            and surrender.

Eighty-eight years old.
        Five decades
of self-obliteration

and you are still here.

ELEGY FOR LAWRENCE HONG

i.

The language I am inventing right now
can only be spoken at sunrise, alone
in kitchens of houses where everyone else is asleep.
In this language, *Hong* is the sound of a slow bronze bell
large enough for a person to hide inside.
Hong is a sound that is heavy, yet light enough
for the air to carry and pass
molecule to molecule over the city.

When the vibrations touch the base of a tree,
they are absorbed through the root system. They grow
into heartwood, hold time in their rings. If the pine-
and birch- and willow-bark is stripped,
and the trees cut into cross-sections,
the disks can be played as records.

They sound like the spokes of your bicycle
spinning in the background as you laugh
at something we can't hear. The records disintegrate
after one use. So we let the trees grow, and trust
your voice is in them.

In this language, *Lawrence* means both friend and the feeling
when the palm of a hand touches very soft grass and is welcomed
into spring.

ii.

The internet is full
of all the pictures your mother has ever taken of you.
 You grin beside your best friend in his profile photos
– so many of them. Like he was preparing to lose you
or never thought he would.
You're in kitchens and restaurants,
parades and living rooms,
sunglasses and bathing suits and inside jokes.

You're at parties I never went to
because there would always be
another time.

And the internet is full of court battles. To release
the marks on your body. The weapon.
How a person can wield himself
against another person
and break him.

The internet wants your body
like a plot device in a crime show
or a story in which
there are answers.

Waiting for the metro five time zones away,
your killer's face shines down from a television,
and no one should have to say
"your killer's face."
He has a name, but I would rather
remember yours.

The city planning you studied. You showed
how a space is made
by being in it.

I will say your name
and hold it. Let it breathe in sunrise
and between the small raindrops
and between the heavy raindrops
and in the space that holds us.

Let the sound of your name
be continuous, and let it mean
the opposite of violence.

You're here.

You're still here.

rain in the cedars
a blackbird's red
shiver

THAT SUMMER

For Margit Rach

whatever the afterlife is or isn't, it must be freer than breathing
through machines. still, that summer I can't see a sunflower
without tearing up, or get through the chorus of "Let Her Go,"
which is everywhere that summer, my mom and I holding

each other in the car. and I cried in Dairy Queen, because
we stopped for fast food that summer we went camping,
and you and Opa helped me catch moths, rescuing them
from spiderwebs, netting the tiny ones in the grass, the ones

that are everywhere once you notice them. and we camped
in the Superstore parking lot, sticky with raspberry juice,
and I dumped handfuls of dirt into the flower vase trying
to give them nutrients, trying to keep that summer alive.

and you made me go to church, but it was okay because
we also saw a bird museum. and we saw a moose, which,
after Googling, it turns out they really are as big as a van
and that's not just how I remember it.

mourning
the dog drops his toys
at my feet

A river sinks through your centre. Water uncoils

arteries – the rhythms of sugar. You curl in radio veils.

Skin remembers stones. The patterns of dishes.

Whose body hesitates? The sediment of mourning

sinks autumn into bone. You drink an orchestra of soil.

In the field of the page

your fibres curl, a struggle

between ecstasies. Your throat loose: a rush

of rice and bells.

INVINCIBLE

for B.

We trekked along the Bow River, Chinatown lights pooling
on the snow. The evening a thin soup of riversalt and pinewind,
inhaling car exhaust and distant ginger. While we were
in the restaurant bathroom, our friends stuck us with the bill
and ran. Left us to emerge into shreds of their laughter
still caught in the door swinging shut behind them.

So we walked too, away together, rare luxury of nowhere to be
but where we were. This stolen blue evening, shadows on snow,
apartment windows quilts of coloured flame, and we talked
of evergreens reabsorbing the city, the mountains rolling
down to cover our small lives. We dated once, as in one date, stilted

and stumbling, hand dropping hand when we saw your aunt –
and then months of discomfort. How long to embrace, for eyes
to hold eyes, how to step away   without leaving. But now
winter is breaking up on the water, icebergs we kick black-booted
to the waves, and the quiet that fills us is comfort, not fear. And then

our phones are ringing, our friends calling us back, and we are
the ones not answering, the ones getting away with something.
I am invincible, I say, a joke for which I've forgotten the context
except that I know you said it back. Our friends calling and calling,
your ringtone fuzzing "This Modern Love" as we walked, listening
all the way through. And I wanted to say, *you're my friend
and I love you*, but I knew

you knew.

I thought the term "histrionic"
came from "hysterical," as in
wandering uterus, as in craziness
a part of the body split off yet
inside it: pulsating   fleshly
and feral. What Aretaeus calls
"an animal within an animal." But,
on further reading, it turns out
"histrionic" comes from "histrio,"
Latin for actor, and has nothing
to do with the uterus. Meaning,
instability is not a trapped animal,
but a context in which one moves,
a way of watching and evaluating
how a body comports itself
across a stage. For example,
when an actor enters from the right
and exits left, an English-speaking
audience will read the character as
somehow off, because they read the
stage like English, eyes flicking
left   then right. The space
between actor and audience bristles,
brushed against the grain, a pause
within a pause which creates
                              tension.
For example,
in a medical context, dialogue
may be misread if a metaphor

does not translate: a figure
of speech becomes psychosis
if, in a different language, the
expression cannot be located
or does not exist. The difference
between metaphor and delusion
is context, not content. How one
translates across language
and space.

But historia is not
psychosis. Is too self-aware,
controlled in how lack of control
is presented. Is *pervasive pattern
of excess, attention seeking, uses
makeup to attract.* Is *quickly
changing* and *shallow.* A character
without depth. *Theatrical.* The issue
isn't the acting, but the badness of
the acting. That she (and 4:1, it's she)
reminds us we are watching a play,
so we sense the gap between actor
and character. Caricature. Caught
in the act. But also, *suggestible.*
Acted upon. A body in the spotlight,
which reminds us there's a spotlight.
Who pleads too obviously to be
believed.

In a Goodreads
review of Iranian-American writer
Porochista Khakpour's memoir,
Sick, one man calls the book *cluster
B bullshit,* cluster B meaning
borderline, narcissistic, antisocial,

or *histrionic*. Meaning, she has put
herself on a stage and knows it.
Controls how she is seen, and can
be seen controlling it. Meaning, she
wants to be believed, and he can
follow her eyes to the wires of her
wanting. Meaning, he believes
she is ill, but that she is ill
incorrectly, so ill she would lie
about illness and not even know
she is lying, yet should know
enough to stop performing.
The histrio *expresses*

    her emotions intensely
yet remains unconvincing.

        She is diagnosed
not by her actions, but by others'
reactions to her actions. By being
cast in a play that doesn't suit her;
how she fails

        to suspend our
disbelief. How she makes us want
to tear down the curtain.[1]

---

1   Upon further research, HPD was one of the diagnoses that emerged when
the category of hysteria was renamed and divided.

Some critics believe Kusama to be performing her mental illness. While this is undoubtedly true, they equate performance with artificiality. According to their theories, her choice to live and work in a psychiatric hospital reflects her desire for publicity, rather than safety. Though Kusama claims to have experienced hallucinations since childhood, critics point out inconsistencies; how she never mentioned these experiences until after meeting with American psychiatrists. They argue Kusama has never valued privacy. That she has constructed galleries to her obsessions, to phalli and food, asked to be photographed nude with her fear.

These critics do not necessarily devalue Kusama. They argue the lens of illness obscures the depth of her work. Her theories of mirror and water, of the image returned fractured and infinite. They argue such thoughtfulness cannot be an illness. That her work stems from structure rather than decay. That illness is antithetical to calculation.

Dots saturate her childhood paintings, as they later do her obliterations. In one, a woman stands in a snowstorm, face and landscape scattered into sky. Polka dots blend/dissolve. The nets appear later, cast across decades, though some early paintings appear retouched to include them.

Kusama destroyed most of her work when she left Matsumoto. Animal glue blackened the air, particles mingling with her breath. Common practice for artists, for whom unshaped imperfection presents a threat to biographic myth.

Her critics concede she has suffered. Admit obsessions, anxiety, insomnia, arrhythmia, suicidal ideation and attempts. Admit her overbearing family, her all-consuming work ethic. How her art is not escape but existence. Her categorization as outsider, as narcissist, as Japanese woman who signed her name to her work; who anticipated the frames of the photographs, and so positioned herself to stare back.

Even though I know David Foster Wallace tried to push the poet Mary Karr out of a moving vehicle, I find comfort in his story "Good Old Neon," in a narrator who can open: *All my life I've been a fraud.*

The narrator, Neil, is not David. It's bad reading to equate the two. I know.

But fallacy or not, one colours the other. Becomes the light by which we read.

In "Good Old Neon," Neil/David describes a person's mind – or their soul, if you believe in that – as a closed room containing everything in the universe: all of time and space. Trying to understand a person, he says, means looking through a keyhole into that room, squinting at the particles of light that fall through.

Meaning, we can never understand each other. But we can understand there is more than what we see, and, in recognizing that lack, make space for empathy. Or at least, stop struggling so futilely to share ourselves in our entirety. Accept we are all mostly unseen.

For a year I took a selfie on my webcam every time I cried. I lifted my laptop above my head, bending my wrists uncomfortably, so that the camera would widen my eyes and avoid the appearance of a double chin. I posted the photos in a Facebook group, where they received more or less likes depending on the angle, on my make-up and clothing, and on the time of day.

Mary Karr begins her memoir, *Lit,* "Any way I tell this story is a lie."

Reading D.T. Max's biography of David, I empathize with him even when he is hurting others. Even when, as a ninth grader, he shoves his sister to the ground and drags her across the muddy, dogshat lawn. I empathize with him because I know there is more to him than this moment, know it hurt him, too, to carry violence inside. Maybe this is empathy in the wrong direction.

I empathize for his sister, too, of course. Not only for the filth but because she lost her brother. Because no matter how much mud, it hurts to look for someone and see only an empty room. I empathize with the family, by which I mean, I understand I cannot understand what they have lost.

When Neil is a teenager, he torments his sister in plausibly deniable ways. How he positions his body in relation to hers when they pass in the hallway, signaling she exists too largely and awkwardly. She stops eating, then resumes, the phase passing without apparent consequence. No one confronts Neil, except his own guilt, listening to his mother's worry through the walls. He returns to this guilt when he explains why he doesn't want to exist.

One could argue this is rumination, not empathy. How he touches his own badness like a comfort.

But that feels harsh. I like Neil, feel like I know him. His desperation makes him seem honest, even when he is calling himself a fraud. Is desperation the same as honesty? Maybe, sometimes, it is close enough?

It is hard not to love the dead, even the fictional dead.

I love Neil for how he knows he is a fraud and how this knowing changes nothing. For how he's aware his confessions are pleas for sympathy and praise, consciously adjusting the angle by which he is viewed. How he tells us that he is trying to present himself as a person who is too hard on himself – but in admitting that, is he being too hard on himself? – but in asking that question, is he manipulating us? I love him because I know the double bind and I haven't found an honest way out, either.

Neil's sister, Fern, isn't really in the story. But then, no one besides Neil is really in the story. It's a claustrophobic forty-something pages, walls of text straining with more than they can hold. It's a story about a man who locks himself inside the room of himself and then explodes it.

I say "a man" and not "a person" not because I believe this double bind to be a strictly male experience. Who doesn't want to be understood? But few women must struggle so adamantly to convince others we are deceitful.

Reading "Good Old Neon," one can't help but wonder if the story is itself an act of manipulation. It answers us, of course, yes, but also that every story is a kind of manipulation, a shifting slant of light, an angle by which we see as far as we can.

When David walked the grounds of Amherst College, he bragged to his friends about the "smell of cunt in the air." Can we dismiss this as a self-conscious performance of machismo? Does that make it any more excusable?

Even though David stalked his ex-girlfriend Mary Karr, followed her five-year-old son home from school.

Even though Mary Karr has written five books of poetry, four books of non-fiction, won the Whiting, PEN, and Pushcart awards, and I'm still calling her *his ex-girlfriend Mary Karr*.

We can't see much of Fern in "Good Old Neon," except that she grows up to be "witchily pretty." I wonder if she also sees herself as a fraud.

In a letter to Elizabeth Wurtzel, David wrote:

> I go through a loop in which I notice all the ways I am – for just an example – self-centered and careerist and not true to standards and values that transcend my own petty interests, and feel like I'm not one of the good ones; but then I countenance the fact that here at least here I am worrying about it, noticing all the ways I fall short of integrity, and I imagine that maybe people without any integrity at all don't notice or worry about it; so then I feel better about myself […] but this soon becomes a vehicle for feeling superior to (imagined) Others […]. I think I'm very honest and candid, but I'm also proud of how honest and candid I am – so where does that put me.

Is acknowledging fraudulence the same as authenticity?

Is desperation?

Even though David climbed the wall of Mary Karr's house when she locked him out.

Even though he threw a coffee table at her.

Even though he put his fist through her car window.

When do we allow cruelty to fascinate us, and when do we cull it from the narrative? Is there another way to angle the light? Whose gaze do we look through or into?

Something I like about Neil is that, in talking about fraudulence, he acknowledges it's not even an uncommon personality type. Isn't *that* at least authenticity? After all, who hasn't had these conversations, variations of trying to line up the room with the keyhole?

Like at the party, when my queer friends and I shaved each other's heads in the bathroom, our movements the movements of people who have been told all our lives we're moving wrong, told we exist too largely and awkwardly. Apologizing when we touch, and touching anyway. *Is this okay?* Running our fingertips down the soft bristly hair, and after my face hurts from shaking, hurts from smiling.

I know that's not the audience Neil means, or David means, but I can relate where I want to relate, right? If the story is meant to be universal, can't I be part of the universe?

"Good Old Neon" is sort of a love story. At least, it's a story about love, in that Neil kills himself because he realizes he is a "yuppie who can't love." Because he is ashamed of how banal that is.

I don't think it's banal. The desire to love makes him more likeable. But then, maybe that was also planned. Yet if love is seeing the room inside others, or trying to see it, to recognize consciousness, isn't that a moral duty, and can't its absence or failure make sense of the story's central crisis?

Weirdly, though, when Neil talks about love, he's less concerned with seeing others than with being seen. Maybe that's what kills him: the self-consciousness, rather than the lovelessness.

The part of the story that explodes the story, when the car hits the wall and the rod of the steering wheel pierces Neil, the part of the story before/during/after Neil dying, he realizes he didn't have to die:

But it wouldn't have made you a fraud to change your mind. It would be sad to do it because you think you somehow have to.

And I hold it even if it wasn't written for me.

In an interview, Karr says of David, "[...] after 20 years of silence about it, at a certain point I feel like I was complicit with somebody who beat my ass."

If telling a story is a lie. If not telling the story is a lie. If we still have to have a history.

In "Suicide's Note: An Annual," Karr writes: *I just wanted to say ha-ha, despite / your best efforts you are every second / alive[.]*

In a draft of "Good Old Neon," David wrote in the corner of the page, *Ghosts talking to us all the time — but we think their voices are our own thoughts.*

So where does that put us?

KUSAMA'S SELF-OBLITERATION

After a short film directed by Jud Yakult, 1967

o.

open to overlap:
        scratches of light
in black paint. circles of crimson and cinnabar
        magnify and vanish, flicker geometric,   then gone.

offscreen, static groans out of key through guitar
                and piano strings. phantasms accumulate,
illegible   procession: spores or gametes,
        black rhizome   lit planetoid

                lightbitten

                        universe.

the camera's eye swallows
another camera.

i.

somewhere in a forest, the pattern becomes fur.
an animal lies in the grass, its body
        too close
                to identify.
Kusama (her hands veined like leaves)
                        touches white circles to the form,
        which at first appears lifeless

but then rises
　　　　　　　　into a horse.

she presses white circles to her red gown.
　　　when she mounts the horse, they are one white-dotted
　　creature
　　　　　　　　　　　　　moving through
　　the woods.

the dots shine like sun through leaves.
the dots shine like stains on film.

the horse dips its head
　　　to taste the long grass
　　　　　　　　　　at the water's edge.
sips from the dark river
　　　which also glows with dots.

　　a figure who may be Kusama walks into the water,
　　　　arms out, her body is a cross draped in fabric.
　　　　　　she floats white ripples in the black tide.

　　she polka dots the lily pads
　　　　urgent perfect circles carried off with the waves.
　　　　she paints the water　　　as it washes itself
black　　the marks she leaves　　no pigment　　but ripple.

a frog leaps
　　　scattering droplets.

Kusama's body is missing frames,
      the absence of motion
          between each motion.
      she moves like a ghost or a spirit
supernatural weaving through the natural.

she lays oak leaves down the back of a resting cat.
she lays oak leaves down the spine of a person
      who lies flat and nude on the soft, damp earth.

the figure stands. she crowns him in leaves.
she buries him in leaves.

         the cat slinks off, glowing with polka dots

disappears into the trees.

ii.

suddenly – skyscrapers – urban glow –
faces honeycombed by shadow.

the bodies sip the light.
the bodies bury themselves in light.

there is paint and there are ears of corn.
there are cellular fractals. there is light shifting
      through water onto skin / sand / anemones.

there are foods and flowers, humans dressing / undressing
   in the half-dark.

clothing or cells or art

androgynous, collaged

people paint each other: primary colours
                    soak skin and fabric.

there are dots. there are branches. veins of humans and plants.

there are membranes.
        the space between them
collapses.

iii.

Kusama eats something.
she does something to the floor
        to create light.

someone is dancing
        or standing in the light
                that dances over them.

iv.

there is affection or violence, bodies crashing
                        into bodies.
joy or fear, hard touch, paint like mud.

there is too much to watch.
the screen crowds / my skin / like a train.
how do we touch
without hurting
        and why.

we move through each other.
I want to believe
this can be gentle.

v.

* 1

---

1   zoom out to a polka dot
        a planet or a cell

A personality disorder is, by definition, an inflexible pattern of thought and behavior that remains stable across time and situations. If the disorder consists of instability, that instability must remain consistent. That is to say, must remain unstable across time and situations.

A person with a borderline personality feels almost everything. Though a person without a borderline personality may also feel that they feel almost everything, in comparison they feel almost nothing. A person with a borderline personality may think they feel nothing, but the feeling of feeling nothing is something they are feeling deeply. They are overwhelmed by feeling, even if it is a feeling of feeling nothing.

To be diagnosed, this unstable, fragmented, or lack of identity must remain stable across time and situations, meaning it must remain unstable, fragmented, or lacking across time and situations. Due to frantic search for identity, one may adopt the identity of a borderline personality. Meaning, one may adopt the identity of unstable, fragmented, or lacking identity. It may be difficult to differentiate a person who truly lacks identity from a person who has adopted an identity of lack.

It may be difficult to discern the difference between what a person feels and what a person believes they feel. Almost every person believes they feel almost everything, but there are different degrees of everything. Some everythings are almost nothings. Some nothings may comparatively be everything. Is to leave the diagnosis to lose an everything? One cannot leave the diagnosis. To be unable to leave is a criterion.

Rejecting the diagnosis of a borderline personality is one indication of a borderline personality. However, if one too readily adopts the identity of a borderline personality, a practitioner should be wary, as this indicates a need for identity, though this may also be a symptom of the illness. Because there is no cure for the illness, those who appear to recover do not meet and have never met the criteria for an illness which must remain stable across time and situations. However, the appearance of recovery may also be a symptom of instability.

I WRITE THE WORD REAL IN RED PEN
REPEATEDLY DOWN MY FOREARM

I comb philosophy essays for nourishment I could better find
    in the fruit bowl
or a conversation.

"The body is a frontier between myself and everything else,"
    writes Walter Ong.
I write that down.

I try to be a proper academic, bingeing vegetable chips in secret.

I write a poem about wanting to be understood by an abstract,
    imagined audience.
S reads it and thinks I am cheating on her.

I write, *I'm not sure if I keep failing to connect to others, or if I'm*
    just greedy
for a level of closeness that doesn't exist.

I guess that is a kind of cheating.

I forget the medication that keeps my body inside my body.

Climbing into S's bedsheets I lecture her about the afterlife. Say:
    there is no such thing
as identity. Say: soon we will have no bodies or boundaries, our
    thoughts dissolved
into one same substance. Say: we are all always already in the
    afterlife and all always
touching and in the end we will all, finally, understand each other.

She tells me to go to the doctor.

I "forget" to eat.

I hand in my poems and am told I use too much crescendo.

In a news article, a 20-year-old begs to be hospitalized, drives
    off a cliff, begs, again,
to be hospitalized. They release her against her will and she dies.
Her family is told this was inevitable.

I attend a lecture about women who have set themselves on fire,
    women who have ripped
at their hair and skin and eyebrows, women who could not stay
    intact.

The experts use words like "chronic" "severe" "disturbance." I nod
    academically.

I imagine a zipper atop my head, yanking it down: undressed,
excessive, disastrous. My nerves raw before a lecture hall of aghast
    faces.

I pick at my cuticles.

At the Pulse vigil, the crowd drains of colour   and then
                                pavement   rising.
I wake to a tunnel of water bottles and hands, to my name in my
    friends' mouths.

I write the phrase "my friends' mouths" and read it. Again.

People are dying and I am writing poems. It's not crescendo because it doesn't stop.

I'm not sure if I believe in an afterlife.

Hélène Cixous: "I do not want the stigmata to disappear. I am attached to my engravings, to the stings in my flesh and my mental parchment. I do not fear that trauma and stigma will form an alliance: the literature in me wants to maintain and reanimate traces."

I need to believe in a different kind of literature.

Richard Siken writes, "I used to think that if I dug deep enough to discover something sad and ugly, I'd know it was something true. Now I'm trying to dig deeper."

I write that down.

I write the word REAL in red pen repeatedly down my forearm.

I read REAL and try to believe it.

I fill the fruit bowl. I text my friend.

"The body is and is and is and has nowhere to go," writes Wislawa Szymborska.

She is talking about torture.

I am trying to talk about continuance.

NARCISSUS GARDEN

for Yayoi Kusama

1966

You arrive uninvited at the Venice Biennale,
lay out at your feet 1500 mirrored balls
so we can look in on ourselves looking in.

You traffic in obsession. Craft landscapes out of duplication,
claim Warhol plagiarized your repetition. Now you reappropriate
yourself: in silver kimono, uninvited at the Venice Biennale,

selling your art piece by piece, cheap *as hot dogs
or ice cream*. Your comparisons so American.
Art to take home and see ourselves in.

The guards ask you to stop. You strip down
to red jumpsuit, lay down in the pool of our gaze:
this strange woman, uninvited at the Venice Biennale.

Was this before or after you leapt from your Manhattan
    window,
bicycle breaking your fall? Neighbours gathered in the alley.
You saw yourself in their eyes looking in.

Erased in a strange country, even your obsessions
reattributed. You could never be seen on their terms.
You invited yourself to the Venice Biennale.

Now you stand, small and smiling in your mass-produced sea,
selling us back to ourselves, cheap. Hold out the ball as crystal
    or future.
Sell us our own eyes back, looking in.

The garden remains when they ask you to leave.
Waves of reflection break and reshape, forever changing the
    space
where you stood, uninvited, at the Venice Biennale,
then left us to look at ourselves looking in.

A SHIRT HUNG OVER A KITCHEN CHAIR

catches light in its stains
and you want to remember this
the way a camera can't

after
you're left with not much
      not nothing

INTERSECTION

My neighbour wears a suit under his raincoat
as he walks to the synagogue.

I wear a hoodie, sweatpants,
the damp silver air, the rain
in the pine trees. I know
the scientific name for sparrows,
but I don't remember what I did this morning.
This spring I can't read autobiographies;
the first person is a paper cup,
leaking.

My mind looks for faces
in shadows and machines;
accidents of light and wires
bend into what I can recognize.
A bottle cap glimmers in the pebbles.
Yesterday I spilled salad on the floor
and spent several minutes debating
whether this was art.

I remember everything I ate two summers ago.
I remember where I was, but not why
or who was there. Laughter twitches,
a muscle memory
that used to hold touch.
An echo of a name
where there is only wind.

The sidewalks by the lilac tree
ache with thoughts of green.
The bottle caps glitter. I walk
with no destination. It feels a trespass:
the cough of wings in my chest.

My neighbour says something
I don't understand, and I say something
I don't remember.

We cross the street like prayers.

Anxiety is a form of autoimmunity. You can't be trusted with your own intentions. I wash my hands and then I think to wash my hands. This is an attempt at silence.
    Adam Dickinson, "Circulation"

From so much self-thinking, I'm now my thoughts and not I.
    Fernando Pessoa, *Disquietude*

i.

A vow is a promise to G-d, which, if spoken, becomes binding.

Judaism forbids wasting time. Therefore, one must always be
    thinking.

Judaism encourages the act of questioning. For example:

If G-d is omniscient, what is the difference between a thought
    and an action?

If a vow is inevitable, why does G-d not simply possess our
    bodies and make us carry out his will?

If G-d is omnipotent and omnipresent, is there no divide
    between G-d
    and our thoughts?

If G-d is thinking us, are our actions his thoughts? Can we
ever belong to ourselves?

Judaism forbids wasting time. Therefore, one must always be
thinking
or allowing oneself to be thought.

ii.

Intrusive thoughts are thoughts which become
trapped in a mind. Circling flies, they bite, repeat,
contradict what a person wants to be or believe.

(Scrupulosity: obsessive moral guilt,
from the Latin word
for a small, sharp stone.)

These thoughts are violent, sexual, sacrilegious,
an annulment
of oneself.
Priests tremble with visions of devil-worship.
Pacifists dream their hands cupped with blood.

The thoughts are not a problem
unless one becomes distressed.
Worry about thinking a thought
tightens its spirals. A virus:

not quite alive, a thought must replicate
inside the living it hollows.

iii.

Before the world, G-d was called Ein Sof:
the absence of an ending.
Or he would have been called that
had there been anyone
to call him anything.

Before the world, every atom was light
and every space an atom.
Being made by omnipotent Being, the light
filled all dimensions, vibrated
at infinite speed. Its brightness
would have burned away the senses
had anyone existed to perceive.

The light left no space
in which a world could exist.

So G-d created the void,
used his omnipotence
to dim his omnipotence.

This was called tsimtsum, reduction.
Or more accurately: tsimtsumim,
these reductions being plural.

G-d quieted
his divine energy
until it was almost imperceptible.
The infinite world
cooled into something
our human minds could touch.

One tsimtsum more
and nothing at all could exist.

iv.

Obsessive-compulsive disorder is a fusion
between thought and action: one mistakes idea
for intent. Images of harm violence the mind.
The thought of murder is a murder.
The thought of sickness a disease.

How does one stopper a thought?
How to silence a fear
of one's own possibilities?
The misaimed knife, the unsnuffed candle,

certainty a room
already burning.

The disorder may correlate with abnormalities
in the medulla oblongata, which signals the call
for shame, danger, fear, guilt, dread, panic.
If the medulla oblongata ceases to self-regulate
when an action is taken to alleviate distress,
stress hormones will continue to flow.

A person becomes trapped, repeating
actions that promise relief. They sanitize
cracked hands, avoid crossing streets. Avoid
their children, their pets, fire, knives, and speech.
Lock themselves into themselves
again. Again. Again. Again. Again.

They withdraw from the world
until they are almost imperceptible.

The disorder is not in action but in thought.
Or not in the thought, but in thinking
about the thought, allowing the thought,
or avoidance of the thought,
to control one's actions.

Similarly, agoraphobia is not the fear
of open spaces, but the fear of losing
control in the space outside oneself:
of being with others, spilling out
of routine: being seen
as one is.

v.

The right-wing Rabbi Wein says shame is essential
to Jewish identity. "The only question that truly arises
is what one should be ashamed about."

He cites the need for humility, Jewish prayers for forgiveness,
David's desperate repentance before G-d.
Yet, philosopher Howard Adelman argues

that guilt and shame are opposites.
That guilt calls for change, and shame
for avoidance.

While guilt is attached to an action,
shame affixes to one's essence:
being rather than doing wrong.

In the garden of Eden, Adam named the animals,
ambitions G-dlike: through speech
he shaped the world,
constructed what could be thought.

Yet he could not name
what went on inside him,
nor look upon his wife, Chavah,
as a complete being,
another consciousness.
Unaware of himself as discrete entity,
he could not name loneliness.

When he bit the fruit, he recognized
the ache that had always existed:
fallible, embodied, separate,
his inner world his alone,
Chavah's world hers.

None of this is sin, says Adelman.
Chavah and Adam were not punished for their acts
but for hiding them.

In Adelman's view, sin is like shame: a negation
of the self.

vi.

In the Book of Judges, Yiptah vows to sacrifice his daughter.

In English, Yiptah is called Jephthah, though Hebrew has no
    sound for "J"
and no sound for "th."

Yiptah was a military leader from the tribe of Menasseh,
a tribe whose descendants have since vanished
into the diaspora.

Somewhere there are people related to him, though they do
not know it.

Yiptah vowed to lead the Children of Israel in battle against
the Children of Ammon.
He vowed that, if he returned victorious, he would sacrifice
the first living thing to emerge from his house.

He led the Children of Israel in battle against the Children of
   Ammon.
He returned victorious.

As he approached his home, his daughter ran out to greet him.

Yiptah tore his clothes and cried.

vii.

Jews who believe in the devil
believe the devil works for G-d.
After all, if G-d is omnipotent,
the devil must be working for him.

viii.

Statistics on obsessive-compulsive disorder
crowd with voids and contradictions.

Brain scans cannot distinguish mental illnesses.
Diagnosis depends on self-report.

No person can fully enter the mind of another,
so diagnosis is an act of faith.
Doctors must trust that patients mean what they say
and are able to communicate it.

It does not account
for how shame
silences shame.

ix.

In battle, we are told G-d went before Yiptah,
an invisible fire, obliterating
all who rose before him.

If G-d did not approve of Yiptah's sacrifice,
why did he lead him to victory?
Why did G-d not immobilize his daughter in the doorway?
Why did G-d not speak out, or not speak in a way

we could comprehend?

According to the Book of Judges, Yiptah's daughter does not
     protest.
She asks for two months to spend with her friends in the
     mountains.
She is a good daughter. She does not argue with her father
or with the G-d who never speaks in this story.

The Book of Judges never gives her name.

x.

Some hypothesize obsessive-compulsive disorder
is no single condition, but a spectrum
of fixations: on body image, morality,
rules, goodness, safety, hygiene, achievement,
exercise, organization – any psychic distress
that results from a thought
that will not leave.

Where does the line lie
between idea and obsession;
faith and scrupulosity;
fixation and delusion;
mind and self?

At what point does a thought
become an illness?

Diagnosis is made by the extent of distress
as reported by the patient. Not the thought itself
but its persistence.

In the tangle of thought,
which threads can we cut
and which knot the core
we call soul
or self
or consciousness?

Without the thoughts we build our lives around
what are we left with?

xi.

The binding of Isaac is central to Jewish identity.
The refusal to sacrifice the human for the divine.
The message that giving up our lives
is not something that is asked.

Human life is holier than laws.
This is why blood transfusions and surgeries are permitted,
although it is forbidden to wound one's body.

In the story of Yiptah, G-d does not roar.
He does not turn the air stony
or freeze Yiptah's raised hand.

G-d does not appear at all
except in Yiptah's words, in his daughter's loyalty.
In the story of Yiptah, G-d is both an absence
and a thought that will not leave.

xii.

We do not know how Yiptah's daughter spent her last days,
why she asked for two months,
or who she spent them with.

We are told she was remembered in annual ceremonies
but do not know the rituals
or why they stopped.

We are only told she was a willing martyr.
Centuries later, Christian scholars applaud her
as a role model for nuns, praise her unflinching fidelity,
how she willingly extracted herself from the world

though it is Yiptah they bestow with sainthood.

xiii.

In experiences of obsessive-compulsive disorder,
one fears that their fears are actually their fantasies.
That one thinks of committing harm
because of desire rather than anxiety.

One fear is that a person will act
out the worst-case scenario
to finally bring an end to the fear
of the worst-case scenario:
hurt oneself to end the fear
of hurting oneself.

The mind runs over and over
its own sharp stones.

To avoid contaminating others,
one may cease speaking, touching,
or allowing oneself to be touched.
Obsessives quarantine themselves
inside their thoughts,
the danger contained

by force if necessary.

They stop crossing the street.
They stop holding their children.

It is a gradual narrowing of the world.

xiv.

In the beginning, G-d created the void
to make space for the world.
In the beginning, G-d gave us his absence.

To those who believe in tsimtsum,
an absence of apparent miracles
is itself evidence

of G-d's unmatched gift.

xv.

The Book of Judges tells the story
of Yiptah's unnamed daughter
in a strangely neutral tone:

And it came to pass at the end of two months
that she returned to her father, who did with her according
to his vow which he had vowed

The words so clear
they bleach out detail:

a face turned directly
into limitless light,

features obliterated.

xvi.

"Israel" means "those who wrestle with G-d."
Did anyone fight for Yiptah's daughter?
The author remains taciturn.

Some scholars say G-d refused to stop Yiptah,
so that he could be made an example
against rash vows.

Some say this story is intended to depict
the moral decline of the Israelites.
To show they had lost their identity.

Some say he did not sacrifice his daughter.
That the particle "ו" (*veh*) does not mean "and," as in modern
    Hebrew,
but "or." That Yiptah had declared that whatever came to
    greet him
would be either burnt as an offering *or* dedicated to G-d.

Today, Jewish scholars mostly agree
that Yiptah's daughter was permitted to live,
though forbidden to marry.
That she was locked in solitary
and perpetual confinement.
This is agreed to be adequate loss.

Rashi believes Yiptah was punished,
afflicted with an illness which caused his limbs to rot
and fall to the earth. No one knows
where the pieces of him are buried
or when we walk over him.

xvii.

It is impossible to know the fatality rate of obsessive-
compulsive disorder.
Not only do many cases go un- or mis-diagnosed,
it is usually comorbid with other conditions.
One cannot ask the reasons of a person
who has ceased to exist.

According to some mental health advocates,
it is unethical to refer to a person as having "committed"
    suicide,
as this language implies both crime and choice. Instead,
one is supposed to say, "died by."

xviii.

Kol Nidre is an Aramaic legal document
spoken once a year as a prayer.

Kol Nidre means "all vows." It opens Yom Kippur,
the Day of Atonement, which begins at night
as Jewish days do.

Kol Nidre states: we renounce all vows we make
between this and the next Yom Kippur.
Let them all be relinquished and abandoned,
null and void.

Rabbis have gone on to clarify
that this invalidation of vows only applies
if one makes the vow without thinking of Kol Nidre.
If one makes a vow insincerely, the vow is considered genuine.

In the 12th century, Rabbi Meir ben Samuel added the words,
"We do repent of them all." Both the vow and repentance
must be intentional.

Kol Nidre has been protested by both Jews and gentiles.
It has been held as evidence that Jews are untrustworthy.
It has been viewed as a catalyst for reckless vows
and impending corruption.

It continues to be sung.

Kol Nidre is sung three times, first almost a whisper. Then
    louder. And louder.

Some sing it more than three times.

The congregation sings it over
and over and over, to sweep in anyone
who arrives late.

xix.

According to Rabbi Moshe Leiv of Sassov,
disbelief can itself shape virtue;
if we cannot turn to G-d for aid
we become responsible for each other.

xx.

In religious communities, obsessive-compulsive disorder
may present as perfectionism in prayer.
Worshippers labour over hymns for hours,
out of fear they have added, subtracted, or misspoken a word,

fear they have slipped into indecent thoughts,
fear they have lapsed into silence,
fear they have ceased to concentrate,
fear at that moment they do not believe in G-d.

Even in a group setting, prayer is private,
less spoken than thought.
Locked in a person, this compulsion
cannot be perceived
except as a distance.

Regarding this problem,
the ultra-orthodox Rabbi Kanievski
says one should simply read the prayer,
continuing on through possible errors.
That this act is sufficient. Imperfection

itself a form of belief.

xxi.

Yiptah's daughter may have been named Seila or she may
have been named Adah.

She may have been named something else entirely.

xxii.

Judaism promises neither heaven nor hell.

Biblical Jews spoke sometimes of Sheol,
a holding realm for the dead,
where souls lose identity
deep underground, regardless

of how they lived on earth.
Through witchcraft, the dead
can converse with the living

but this practice is forbidden.

Modern Jews reject these views.
Some believe at the end of days
eternal life will lift our bodies:

muscle and flesh will wake our bones,
our veins become vines to bind us
back to our lifeblood.

The earth will open
and our loved ones pour forth
back into our arms.

The ancient temple priests denied this.

The Kabbala speaks of reincarnation,
Maimonides of souls as particles of G-d.
After thousands of years, scholars continue
to argue over heaven, hell, and nonexistence,

but Jews rarely prioritize these discussions.
Ethical debates center on action over belief,
this life over the next. The questions of how

we can live in this world
as though it is enough.

INSOMNIA

Thoughts cannot hurt you. When flies settle on the ceiling,
don't listen to the fever of their wings. Honesty
does not have to be a knife.

When you check your reflection, use the window. A sheet
of glass and silver won't show you as you are. Look to stars
and smog, swaying hands of trees, traffic burning green
against the night. The age of sky above shell-grey streets.

Trace the shape of your hand to remember you are not a bird.
Your bones are not empty. When the beat of carbon and marrow
moves in your limbs, listen. Walk yourself loose
from steel bands of a fracture. You can't seem to hold
your ribs closed, but your chest does not break. The air
is not the color of a migraine. Smudge the list off the back
of your hand, the bruised ink of unfinished tasks.

Birds are not calling out your failure. They are calling
each other home.

SOMETHING LIKE LIVING

[…] most frightening of all, that we may be real or imaginary. Or *and*.
Ray Hsu, "Where To Begin"

Because these pauses are supposed to be life
John Ashbery, "Grand Galop"

CRACKS

I think you understand porosity
        How a self can be
        a poorly-sealed window
        letting in both birdsong
                and rot

I think you understand
these thin membranes
These cracked foundations
That I want to give you something
                that lasts

That I wanted to tell you how
      in your arms
            in the white space of your kitchen
I felt safety at an intensity like tears. The knots in my shoulders
opened at your palms
             and I thought, *nothing*
                    inside me
                    will hurt you

I held that. Under my skin like a promise
I hold that

      Opposite of fear
We pull each other
      into each other

      and make this enough
The furniture in now-our kitchen
The chairs you built yourself
Cookies only slightly burned
      The space I've cleared off the table
          so we can sit

Though I don't always know how to fit
inside my skin, I hope you know

                  I want this

Us, standing, here
      Our legs in a forest
          of dog-gnawed chair legs

Cobwebs kicked off our shins
the old fear tangled
with our socks in the corner

This bareness and this glitter
      of dust in the lowering sun
These bodies of air and hemoglobin
mostly water, and even more
            empty space

that allow us
      to touch
      and hold
      and speak: we too
are capable of beauty

I am learning to be where I am.

TOMATOES AND VINEGAR

Balsamic soaks the bread,
                    bright dark through olive oil.
Cucumbers crunch in their thin skins.

We're home: this is ours,
                    belonging if not owning.

Burble of conversational catch-up,
            the hours between us and back again.
Burble of coffee in the pot
                    waiting to refill our mugs.

Sugar and air, these substances our cells
                                have built into bodies.
        The spaces we fill
                        with what we've found.

                    This place we've made:
animal hair, and storms that shake our windows,
            scuffed hardwood, and dishes always to be done,
            and days
                    that don't stop

        but sometimes slow

until   we can almost hold,

                    across years and time zones,

this taste of sunlight and rain.
This talk like breath.

Hand over hand, water runs warmth across our fingers
as we scrub away the day's soup and butter, salt and sweet
    still ringing in our mouths.

I kiss your neck.
The kitchen window deepens
    our summer into gold.

Light, dragonfly-winged,
ornaments the rusted rail of our balcony,
where we ate cookies dark with cocoa
    and chipped with white chocolate
and drank the deep sunlight of oranges.

You reminded me how to recognize low blood sugar,
stroked my hand until black sparks left my vision
and sky and cityline returned
    and the deep green grass.

We hold each other like light.
I slip into myself
        unafraid.

Speech trips my tongue,
an unpracticed instrument
whose song I long to share
    with you.

You brush the spices
from your countertop,
     turmeric raining
        past your palms.

The room fills with evening, white walls
     gone to gallery of shadows:
indigo   shale   lilac   plum.

We take the night
     into our mouths
soft-skinned
        open

January grass
our dog is impatient
when I stop to look

We argue about the ending. Hopeful, you say. How *choose life*
changes from sarcastic to sincere. I say, Bitter. A stripping of
sarcasm, yes, but not irony, and under that, the raw wires are
desperate. The implied *Because this is all there is. There is
no other way.* The longing is constant, no trapdoor into
something more.

I don't think of it that way, you say.

The credits unspool. We sip our sangria, spoon out the bright cubes
of kiwi and peach I sliced in for vitamin C. Wash bare the bottles,
then head for bed. I guillotine a sleeping pill, press its sand to my
tongue, lay down in the curve you warm around you. You click the
lamp and my drugged vision flickers. Dark petals spin into pixels
on the ceiling. I lie in my body, pulsing.

I feel different from everyone around me, I tell you in the dark,
pressing hard into your arms as you hold me inside myself.

> [My shoulders tighten. I'm waiting
> for a fight, for shouting and tears and the
> closeness   that comes after]

Well, not everyone. Ninety-five percent.

I think most people feel that way.

Yeah. That's probably true.

I don't say: the other five percent upset me. Like we're auditioning for the same role and I haven't had time to practice.

I'm scared, I say.

Why, you say.

I don't know. School.

You don't have to go to school.

I know. I want to.

Things will be easier once you graduate.

I don't want easy.

You turn away. I don't say: I slept fourteen hours last night and expect to do the same tonight. I don't say: I think I'm becoming a person who sleeps all day, and then stumbles through the apartment, clunking like an argument.

I don't remind you of when we watched that documentary about Rudy Giuliani. How they tried to say he did some good things, that he got the drugs off the street, and I got mad, said the drugs were a side-effect, that he hated the homeless, the gay clubs, the mentally ill, wanted the margins swept out of sight. Chased us out, locked us up, left the emptiness behind.

And then I'm talking about emptiness again. How it bonds easily, how it's like, what's it called, the one that's not a noble gas. The kind that needs electrons, fixes itself to whatever it can get. If it's not drugs, it's housework, or food or sex or starvation, or academia, or the stock market, or, or, or et cetera.

You know, I know. But I repeat the conversation in my head, run over the ridges of the same anger, because, it's just ... I don't know what the alternative is.

Not when "moderation" is a sleep-drunk zombie stumble. When stability sounds too much like the month I thought I could make myself love him, if I just paid less attention to how I felt.

Then in the dark: It will be okay, you say. I used to feel that way. Talk it over with your therapist.

I just feel lonely.

You won't always.

We're different people.

Is that bad?

No.

We hold onto each other as sleep covers us. I don't want to be here, but I'd rather be here than anywhere else, and I want to be with you even if that means being me.

You're gone by the time I wake up at noon. Mouth grainy, bittered with medicinal sleep. The day is bright and heavy.

The dog needs to be walked.

first argument
the space at my back
is cold

ON COMPROMISE

i.

So I make you poems and casseroles. I find the gnawing
thing inside me and feed it spinach and television. I walk
the dog, let her bite at my ankles because saying "no"
in a firm voice sounds too much like yelling. Almost enough

is more than most people have. Right? And besides, I want
to want this, and isn't that almost the same as wanting it?
The question would seem to answer itself. But what about:
Try. Isn't that also almost an answer? And haven't we read

enough to stop believing in closure? Can love be calibrated
by how much you're willing to give away? That Christmas
story: your lack of time, my chilly head,

this embarrassment of gifts.

ii.

Later, I learn you don't like casseroles or poetry. That you
just wanted me to feel useful.

We argued again, this time about greed versus hunger. Whether
   a good enough life
can ever be. You say the housewife character was selfish, and
   I say she was, but
that she had to be, that it's okay to have a self, to have a centre

and then we're not talking again.

Pain is a dull word, but I don't know how else to name the people
we're making each other: mutual martyrdom and then yelling
in taxicabs, none of our friends calling us back.

At nights I walk the dog, long black rain beating my long black
coat, posing my moodiness into music video. Shirley Manson's
"Even Though Our Love Is Doomed," because subtlety has never
been my strong point. She sings, *you're the only one worth
dying for,* which actually isn't what I feel, though I do relate

when she sings that she is *desperate for some kind of spark,
some kind of connection.* I don't know what it means
that we equate living with its opposite. It's been years
since I realized that when I said *obliteration*
I meant something like *understanding* or *closeness.*

In *The Hours,* the blank-eyed housewife checks herself into a
   hotel room
with a bottle of pills. Years later she resurfaces, saying, *It would
be wonderful to say you regretted it. But what does it mean
to regret when you had no choice?*

That's not me, though. Maybe it was. Sixteen, cutting my own hair
in the bathroom sink. Or eighteen, or nineteen, or twenty-two.
   Okay, maybe
I'm still the same, still don't know what "future" means, except that
I am moving through it, and that makes it stranger and easier to
    believe in.

After we've talked and argued, passed through silence, and I've
    packed my bags, you text
when I am standing on my friend's doorstep.

You said you would love me no matter what. Liar.

But I meant this: I wanted that.

I was where I was, and then I moved.

new year's morning
washing the bonfire
from my hair

DRUMHELLER

For Adèle Barclay

It is different to be here on purpose

Rae Spoon on the stereo
Leopoldine Core's furious poem
pencilling moon into empty sky
We pass a field of calves

Eating corn nuts on the gas station curb
watching a pair of geese ascend
past McMansion scaffolding

We plunge deeper, back
into highway hum
past backyards where I wrote

voice into mouth
branching possibles of conversation
ghosts into walls of my Oma's house
amidst snap-peas and zucchini flowers

The earth spreads out with nothing
to block the sky

We park in the shadow
of an artificial dinosaur

A child in a purple bathing suit
pours water from a clear plastic cup
toddling purposefully
around the edges of a fountain

The pavement darkens with ritual
as she wills the circle to touch
end to end

and given the choice
I would probably ask
or at least agree
to be born

creeksong
a bluebell balanced
on its stem

BLANK

.

I gave myself diets as something to do. I thought, when I am a good person, I will be able to levitate. I didn't use the word levitate. Didn't try to be the center of attention. I waited to be able to slip off my skin. I believed in reincarnation. I got a job as a waitress, polished glassware until my fingerprints blistered. I said I did not feel it.

My relationships kept ending. They said I was boring. Said I was passive-aggressive. Or just passive. Said I could not take care of myself. That my emotions did not make sense, or I could not explain them in a way that made sense. I stayed up until I saw creatures moving under my skin. I slept until afternoon and then stared at the walls. I lied about being drunk because it was easier to explain. People passed though me without touching.

I decided I did not want to be a good person. I picked up my phone and threw it at the kitchen floor. I picked up my body and threw it in a snow bank. I took the worst parts of myself and threw them in a poem. I called the poem "love me," but couldn't say it out loud. I called the poem "hate me," but couldn't keep my voice steady. I called the poem "manipulation." It wasn't a good poem but I showed it to everyone. I wanted to fight with my friends but couldn't stop apologizing, and they didn't realize I was trying to be rude. I wanted someone to be wrong.

I wanted to cut edges out of opposites. To see myself outlined sharply on a backdrop. I wanted my friends to be mad at me, but they just asked if I was okay. I said yes. I thought, "I don't exist," or, "I don't exist yet," but I thought it very quietly. I went to parties and drank all the wine and ate all the Oreos and didn't talk to anybody. I went home early. I shut the door and heard everyone talking, but they did not talk about me.

Snow swirled on the air. I thought, everyone will be okay without me. The thought did not hurt. A white room opened inside me. The room was very still and very quiet. As I walked, snow struck the asphalt, made crinkling sounds. A taxi pulled up and I stepped in. I did not have to save money anymore.

I wanted to be warm. I put my body in warm clothes. I put my body in my bed. I woke up crying. Days in a row, I woke up crying. Or I woke up okay, then, crying. I thought I would dehydrate. I thought, there was an ending, and I missed it. Yet I kept leaking out. Whatever the I was.

The days laid out bare on the window, bled light into one another. I moved my body between rooms. I washed its hair. Sometimes. Fed it oranges and coffee, took it to the store. I looked inside it for the white room, but the door was locked. Then there was no door, just blank walls. Then something else.

I woke clawless, stilled and hollowed in that way
that lets the light in. I spent an hour debating
whether to drink coffee, couldn't remember what
I enjoyed besides coffee; so I paced, scrubbed dishes,
let sediments of light drift towards my eyelids.

No one else in the house was awake. I had three hours
before my appointment, three hours to spend with myself.
I was afraid, or another emotion I couldn't identify.
I watched YouTube, practiced the dialogue of casual
conversation. The air in my bedroom moved slowly.
I made the bed. Nico stretched at the edge, let me pet him.
Morning glowed his eyes green. I took pictures with my phone
but he kept blinking.

In the quiet, my body was a lengthening vibration. A wine-
glass buzz that had settled into something else. Steady
pulse of a bass line. Last week piled in the corners of the room:
cat hair and unopened packages, a bruise muddying my right knee.
The clothes I'd discarded buried the floorboards.

I remembered a hole in my chest filled with static, anger
at myself for making you mad at me. But the "you" doesn't
fit you, becomes a symbol, metal screech against eardrums.
All the soft noise sharpened inside me. But when I try
to walk backwards through the days, to trace your face
and the source of your anger, a blank space rises to meet me.

An argument too small for memory. Something like,
I said I was going to bed, and you didn't beg me to stay.
Or I joked I was ugly, and you laughed, so I became ugly.
Or I made myself replaceable, and was demolished
when you found me replaceable. Or I woke up alone
and that was all. We were two friends, and I had no words
to ask how to live inside myself.

A room of sun and books, cat hair and unopened envelopes.
The space in the air where an apology may or may not fit.
It's my favorite joke: thank goodness *that's* never happening again.
When what I mean to say is, please understand. I am tired
of putting my organs under glass and demanding,
"take this." I can't watch those movies anymore,
where the loved ones push the guardrails, fish each other out
of the pool, insist no one can leave. You can leave. One day,
I will be able to say that with you in the room.

You are at work or sleeping behind a closed door,
a threshold I cannot cross. Our lives stretch separate paths
across the same floorboards. Beneath the same dust.

We can leave our hair in the corners or clear it away.
Put posters over the spackle, hang them crooked
and unironic. I will move myself inside the space of a day,
towards you or another, or towards conversation.

Again I am learning to be where I am. To make a mess
my own.

Some of these poems have previously appeared in publication, often in slightly different form.

"white infinity net" appeared in *Lemon Hound*.

"Petrocan" appeared in *The Goose*.

"broken sunrise" and "the old woman's hands" appeared in *Frogpond*.

"room without walls" appeared in *Prism*.

"through the train window" appeared in *Acorn*.

"shadows on the moon" appeared in *Matrix*.

"in human rooms" appeared in *Room*.

"Insomnia" was featured as the University of Calgary "Poem of the Season" and received an honourable mention in the Tom Howard/Margaret Reid poetry contest.

"a shirt hung over a kitchen chair" appeared in *Foliate Oak* under the title "this is one of those moods."

"Book of Judges" appeared in *To Be Decided**.

"creeksong" appeared in *Modern Haiku*.

"Acts of Daily Living" appeared in *Headlight*.

This collection draws its title from a theory of immune system functioning proposed by Polly Matzinger in 1994. The theory posits that, rather than targeting unfamiliar material, the immune system is structured to attack anything it perceives as dangerous, which may include one's own body. Conversely, the immune system may welcome and incorporate foreign material that it does not perceive as a threat.

The opening epigraph is taken from Carrie Fisher's personal Twitter, @carrieffisher.

"white infinity net" remixes phrases from Yayoi Kusama's autobiography, *Infinity Net*, translated by Ralph McCarthy, and from Jill Bolte-Taylor's interview with Guy Raz on National Public Radio.

"Performance Piece: On the Crowd" is based on Marina Abramovic's "Rhythm 0," a six-hour performance at Studio Morra, Naples in 1974. The poem incorporates quotes from the artist's statement and lists the objects Abramovic presented to be used on her at the audience's discretion. The phrase "catalogue of harms" comes from Erin Moure's collection of poetry and theory, *Furious*. The Tori Amos lyrics come from "Cornflake Girl" off the album *Under the Pink*. The poem also alludes to her album *Little Earthquakes*, particularly the song "Me and a Gun."

Italian Stallions is a 2008 romance novel by Karin Tabke and Jami Alden (thank you, Google) (I anticipate some interesting ads now).

"Green Halo" incorporates information from Amanda Kelly's article, "What's that green light in Montreal's sky?" published on GlobalNews.ca on July 4th, 2014.

"Strangelove Syndrome" draws on the article "The alien hand syndrome" by Ragesh Panikkath, Deepa Panikkath, Deb Mojumder, and Kenneth Nugent, published in *Baylor University Medical Center Proceedings* 27:3 (2014).

"borderline: talk" is a cut up/erasure of the Wikipedia article on Borderline Personality Disorder and its associated talk page. Wikipedia members frequently descend into "edit wars" on the article, due to shifting diagnostic criteria, contradictory research findings, and ethical issues around how to discuss symptoms without contributing to internet contagion.

"Ode to Pessoa" quotes from numerous poems by Fernando Pessoa. I have used the translations by Richard Zenith, which can be found in his book *Pessoa & Co.*

The quotes from Emily Dickinson come from *The Gorgeous Nothings,* a compilation of Emily Dickinson's envelope poems, edited by Jen Bervin and Marta Werner with contribution by Susan Howe.

"Alexithymia" references Bessel van der Kolk's *The Body Keeps the Score,* Peter Steggals' *Making Sense of Self-Harm,* and an interview between Marianna Pogosyan and Batja Mesquita entitled "How Culture Shapes Emotions," published online on *Psychology Today.*

Lawrence Hong was a student at the University of Calgary, an incredibly active volunteer with numerous arts, urban planning, and LGBTQ groups, and a welcoming, funny, and kind presence around the Q Centre. His efforts helped many people see that this world has a place for them. He will always be remembered with love by his friends and family.

"Let Her Go" is a song by Passenger.

"This Modern Love" is a song by Bloc Party.

"Performance Piece: On Historia" includes quotes from the third, fourth, and fifth editions of the *Diagnostic and Statistical Manual of Mental Disorders* and from Sharon C. Ekleberry's *Integrated Treatment for Co-Occurring Disorders: Personality Disorders and Addiction.*

"Performance Piece: On Sincerity" includes quotes from D.T. Max's biography of Wallace, *Every Love Story is a Ghost Story*; David Foster Wallace's "Good Old Neon" (published in *Oblivion*); Mary Karr's *Lit*; and Karr's NPR interview with Robin Young.

"Iatrogenesis" appropriates (and approximates) some language from the fourth and fifth editions of the *Diagnostic and Statistical Manual of Mental Disorders*, but is primarily a synthesis of arguments encountered both online and in psychiatric literature. Despite being defined as incurable, a large proportion of those who meet the criteria for BPD eventually recover, with some estimates saying that 80% of former patients no longer meet diagnostic criteria ten years down the line. However, although treatment is often effective, many clinicians refuse to treat patients diagnosed with this condition due to its perceived incurable nature.

"I write the word REAL in red pen repeatedly down my forearm" includes quotes from Walter Ong's *Orality and Literacy,* Hélène Cixous' *Stigmatatexts,* Richard Siken's "Black Telephone," and Wislawa Szymborska's "Tortures."

The young woman who died after being refused hospital care was Hailey Baker, a resident of Newfoundland.

In "Book of Judges," the line "One more tsimtsum more and nothing at all could exist" is taken from Tzvi Freeman's article, "What is Tsimtsum? - Presence Through Absence," which appeared on Chabad.org. "Book of Judges" also references work by Howard Adelman, specifically his writing in "Shame and Humiliation in Judaism Versus Christianity," posted on HowardAdelman.com, as well as Berel Wein's article "Shame and Shameful," posted on RabbiWein.com. Information about obsessive-compulsive disorder is drawn from Avigdor Bonchek and David Greenberg's "Compulsive Prayer and its Management," which appeared in *The Journal of Clinical Psychology* 65:4 (2009), as well as from David Greenberg and Gary Shefler's "Ultra-Orthodox Rabbinic Responses to Religious Obsessive-Compulsive Disorder," which appeared in *The Israel Journal of Psychiatry and Related Sciences* 45:3 (2008). Biblical quotes and references are drawn from the New International Version.

The phrase "something like living" comes from John Ashbery's "Self-Portrait in a Convex Mirror."

"After *Trainspotting*" refers to the film *Trainspotting* (1996, directed by Danny Boyle) and paraphrases from Marya Hornbacher's *Wasted:* "And yet, you are all that you have, so you must be enough. There is no other way."

"After *The Hours*" refers to *The Hours* (2002, directed by Stephen Daldry) and quotes both that film and the Garbage song "Even Though Our Love Is Doomed" off the album *Strange Little Birds*. It also references the lines from Margaret Atwood's *Morning in the Burned House*, "No one / ever told you greed and hunger / are not the same."

Information on Yayoi Kusama comes from Heather Lenz's 2018 documentary *Kusama - Infinity,* produced by Heather Lenz, Dan Braun, Karen Johnson, and David Koh.

ADDITIONAL INFORMATION ON KUSAMA COMES FROM:

Jujyfruits. "Kusama's Self-Obliteration (Jud Yakult, 1967)." Online video. *YouTube*, May 6, 2013. Web. Retrieved Dec 2, 2016.

Kusama, Yayoi, Jaap Guldemond, Franck Gautherot, Seung-Duk Kim, Diedrich Diederichsen, Midori Yamamura, and Lily Van Der Stokker. *Yayoi Kusama, Mirrored Years*. Dijon: Les Presses du Réel, 2009. Print.

Louisiana Channel. "Yayoi Kusama Interview: Earth is a Polka Dot." Online video. *YouTube*, Jan 8, 2015. Web. Retrieved Dec 7, 2016.

ACKNOWLEDGMENTS

It is impossible to thank all of the people whose wisdom, kindness, and generosity have made me a better writer and person. This book could not have come into being without you.

For all the artists and volunteers who have worked tirelessly to make Calgary and Montreal's writing communities more vibrant, welcoming places; for all my teachers who encouraged my writing, reading, and learning in all its forms; for all my friends who listened when I needed it, whose warm words and excellent company and beautifully bizarre senses of humour (long live Buzz Knucklebones) help me find joy and meaning; for my family, who always believed in me and encouraged my creativity; for everyone who speaks the truth of their experiences, and for everyone who is willing to listen – this is for you. Thank you.

Thank you Carolyn Smart, editor extraordinaire, for your attentiveness, enthusiasm, and willingness to read *a lot* of drafts. These poems are much better because of you.

Janine Chan, for over a decade of encouragement, constructive criticism, and, most of all, friendship. I am always impressed and inspired by your intelligence, thoughtfulness, and compassion. And cat photos.

Mona'a Malik, work buddy and brilliant author, for believing in me and helping me to actually sit down and get these poems written (and who was often sitting across from me working on her own writing as I did so).

Thank you to my cohort in Concordia's creative writing MA program. Your writing is challenging, politically charged, and deeply creative, and pushed me to become a better writer and thinker.

Thank you Sheri-D Wilson, mentor and friend, whose incredible dedication and generosity have been instrumental in both my development as a poet and in shaping Calgary's creative community as a whole. For over a decade, you have helped me to see the possibilities in poetry, to study the rich history of this art form, and to find my voice, my confidence, and my honesty.

Thank you Stephanie Bolster, whose dedication to her students goes above and beyond the very concept of above and beyond. Your amazing teaching and generous feedback have challenged me to research more extensively, think more deeply, write more truthfully, and to trust that I have something worth saying. Thank you for helping me believe that there is a place for me.

Thank you to my MA supervisor, Mary di Michele, for your thoughtful feedback on these poems, and for sharing your expansive knowledge of form, translation, and poetic history. You taught me to listen more closely to the music embedded in the structure of the poem, and to grant space for the words to sing.

Thank you to Rivka Caplan and family, and to the legacy of Mervin Butovsky, for helping fund my education at Concordia University through the Professor Mervin Butovsky Memorial Scholarship. Thank you to the family of Carlyle Norman for sponsoring the Carlyle Norman Scholarship for Emerging Artists, which allowed me to attend the Banff Centre, where much of this manuscript was completed.

Thank you to my cohort at the Banff Center in summer 2017. I was inspired and healed by your stunning creativity, thoughtful conversations, and spontaneous dinosaur road trips. Thank you Karen Solie, Ocean Vuong, and Collette Bryce, for your spot-on feedback and for granting me permission to open the door of the poem and let the wildness out.

Thank you Danielle Bobker, Rachel Shabalin, Crina Bondre Ardelean, Melanie Boyd, Hannah Muszynski, Brittany Briscoe, Helen Lin, Hunter Loubert, Kristen Goodall, Marie Gustafson, Weyman Chan, Bethan McBreen, and everyone else who has supported this work over the years. Thank you Mark Abley and all of the other fantastic people at McGill Queen's University Press who brought this book into reality. Thank you to my brother, Mischa, and my dog-brother, Erik, for brightening my life even when you debate my political opinions or lick my notebooks (I will leave it to your imagination who does which).

Finally, thank you to my parents for supporting my creativity and for always nurturing my interest in reading, writing, and learning. Love you.